OFFICER WOOF! WOOF!

Police Dogs Book for Kids
Children's Dog Books

Speedy Publishing LLC
40 E. Main St. #1156
Newark, DE 19711
www.speedypublishing.com
Copyright 2017

All Rights reserved. No part of this book may be reproduced or used in any way or form or by any means whether electronic or mechanical, this means that you cannot record or photocopy any material ideas or tips that are provided in this book.

DOGS that have been trained to assist police officers in solving crimes are known as police dogs, or K9 officers. Using their bravery and unique skills they have saved many lives. They are known to be watchful, loyal, as well as protective of their officer partners and are deemed to be a vital and irreplaceable part of most police departments. In this book, you will be learning about what it takes to become a police dog and how they are able to assist the police department.

THE EARLY HISTORY OF POLICE DOGS

Since the Middle Ages dogs have been assisting law enforcement personnel. The villages would use money for maintaining a parish constable's dog that would typically be used for hunting down the outlaws. Dogs were also used in France during the 14th century. In Scotland, bloodhounds used in law enforcement were referred to "Slough dogs". The term sleuth (detective) is derived from the term slough.

A K9 POLICE OFFICER STANDING WITH HIS PARTNER

During London's rapid urbanization in the 19th century, public concern was increasing about growing lawlessness, which became way too massive to be dealt with using existing law enforcement. Private associations then formed to assist with combating crime. Night watchmen were being hire to guard premises. They would be provided with dogs and firearms to protect against criminals.

FAMOUS CASES

During the 1880s, Sir Charles Warren utilized bloodhounds to assist with tracking down the serial killer known as Jack the Ripper.

CHARLES WARREN

It was in 1889 that K9's were used for policing by Sir Charles Warren, who was Commissioner of the Police of London. His multiple failures in identifying and capturing Jack the Ripper had earned him lots of criticism by the press, which included being criticized for not utilizing bloodhounds in tracking this serial killer.

Soon, he had two bloodhounds trained in performing a simple tracking test from a scene of one of the killer's crimes. Results were disappointing as one of the dogs bit the Commissioner and both dogs then ran off, and the police had to then search for the dogs.

BLOODHOUND

Dogs started to be utilized on a larger scale in Continental Europe. In Paris, police started using dogs to protect against criminal gangs roaming at night, however, in 1899, it was the Ghent, Belgium police department the first introduced an organized police dog service program. Quickly, these programs spread to Germany and Austria-Hungary.

It was in Germany that the original scientific developments occurred with experiments with training and breeding of the dogs. The German Shepherd Dog was chosen by the German Police to be the best breed for police work and the first dog training school opened in Greenheide in 1920. The dogs were trained systematically for obedience and respect to their officers as well as the tracking and attacking of the bad guys.

GERMAN SHEPHERD

LABRADOR RETRIEVER

The North Eastern Railway Police located in Britain were among one of the first departments that utilized police dogs by using them to stop thefts at the docks located in Hull in 1908. Railway police, by 1910, had started experimenting with using other breeds including German Shepherds, Doberman Pinschers, and Labrador Retrievers.

TRAINING

In order for a police department to consider using a dog, the dog has to pass a basic obedience training court and they have to obey commands from their handler without any hesitation. This provides the officer with complete control over the amount of force that a dog should use against a criminal. In Europe, dogs are trained using the country's native language.

MAN IS TEACHING AND TRAINING A DOG

Initially, the dogs are trained using this language for its basic behavior making it easier to learn new commands/words, other than retraining the canine to learn new commands. This differs to a popular belief that canine officers are trained using a different language so that the suspect will not be able to issue a command to the canine against its officer.

In law enforcement, dogs can be trained to either be "dual purpose" or "single purpose". The dual purpose dog are more common than single purpose dogs which primarily are used for tracking, personal protection, or backup. Dual purpose dogs do the same things as single purpose dogs, but also have the ability to detect narcotics or explosives.

DOG SNIFFING A SUSPICIOUS PACKAGE FOR DRUGS

DOG IN OPERATION OF EXPLOSIVE SEEKING

However, they can't be trained to detect both since the dog does not have the ability to advise the officer whether it found narcotics or explosives. In the United States, once a narcotics dog alerts the officer that it has found something, the officer then has reasonable suspicion for searching what the dog has alerted him to, such as a vehicle or bag, without having to obtain a warrant.

WHAT TYPES OF CANINE OFFICERS ARE THERE?

Today, canine officers are trained for specific tasks. You might call them "experts in their field".

TRACKING DOG IN THE WOODS

Some specific canine officer roles are listed here:

TRACKING – K9 officers who are specialized in tracking utilize their strong sense of smell in tracking missing persons or criminal suspects. They are typically trained for several years and are able to find the most astute criminal. Many suspects would be able to escape from police without the use of these tracking dogs.

SUBSTANCE DETECTORS – These K9 officers utilize their sense of smell in assisting the police, however, it is different than how it is used by tracking dogs. Substance K9s focus on detecting a certain substance. Some might be specialized in bomb recognition or explosives recognition. They are not only trained in finding the explosive, they are also trained on how to respond as well as letting their partner know where it is located.

DRUG DETECTION DOG AT THE AIRPORT

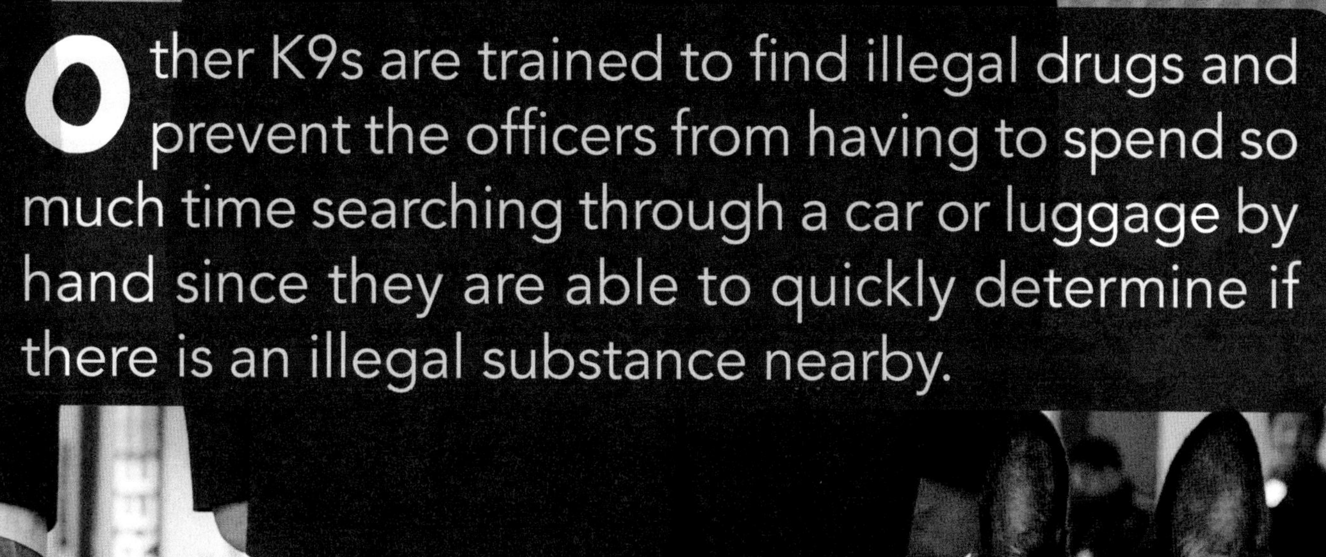

Other K9s are trained to find illegal drugs and prevent the officers from having to spend so much time searching through a car or luggage by hand since they are able to quickly determine if there is an illegal substance nearby.

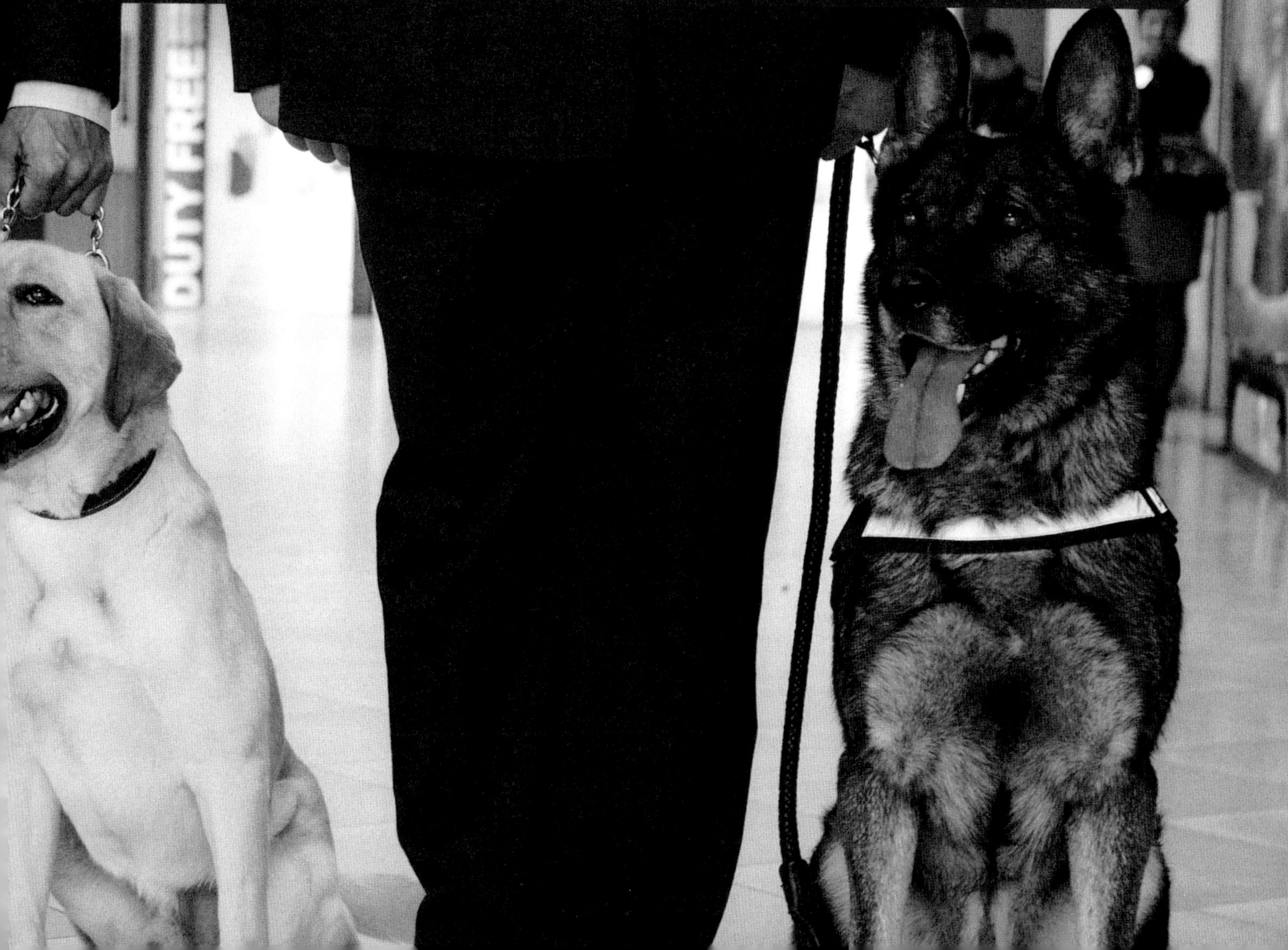

PUBLIC ENFORCEMENT – These K9s work with the officers to maintain order. The K9 might chase a criminal down and hold them until the officer arrives, or they might just simply guard an area, such as a prison or jail, ensuring that suspects do not escape.

CADAVER DOGS – While it might seem a bit gross, these K9s are trained to find dead bodies. They are trained well to do this, and it plays an important function within the department.

POLICE DOG

DACHSHUND

WHAT ABOUT MY DACHSHUND?

Your Dachshund might be a fabulous dog, but more than likely would not be a terrific fit to be a police dog. K9s have to have extremely specific and special training. Many breeds can be trained as K9 officers. The breed used will often depend on the type of work they will be performing.

The Belgian Malinois and German Shepherds are a couple of the most popular breeds, even though Beagles (great for detecting drugs) and Bloodhounds (great for tracking) are also popular. It doesn't matter what the breed, the training of K9s starts when they are still puppies.

BELGIAN SHEPHERD PUPPIES

WHAT HAPPENS TO THE K9 OFFICERS ONCE THEY RETIRE?

Typically, K9 officers are treated as heroes and often they will go live with their human officer partner. They already spent several years with their partner and see them as family, so this is a great option for the K9 and the officer.

GERMAN SHEPHERD DOGS

This is known to be one of the more popular dog breeds in the United States. They are known to be strong, friendly, loyal, and protective.

HOW BIG DOES A GERMAN SHEPHERD GET?

They are large dogs and typically grow to be about two feet tall at their shoulder blades and weigh somewhere between 55 and 95 pounds. They have large ears and usually stand straight up. Typically, they are longer than they are tall and usually very well-proportioned and muscular looking.

WHAT DOES THEIR COAT LOOK LIKE?

Their coat can by just about any color, but you will find German Shepherds with coats that are reddish and black or tan and black. They can also be all sable or all black. Their coat consists of a double coat, which will keep them warm in colder climates. They shed their outer coat all year round. The coat is mostly medium in length, but there is a German Shepherd variety that does have longer hair.

GERMAN SHEPHERDS AS WORKING DOGS

Originally, these dogs were bred to be working dogs and primarily used for herding sheep and protecting them from predators. They are used today widely as police dogs and sometimes as military dogs. In addition, they are great scent dogs and can be trained for sniffing out bombs, drugs, and for search and rescue missions as well.

GERMAN SHEPHERD PUPPY

GERMAN SHEPHERDS AS PETS

German Shepherds are known to be one of America's favorite pets since they can be great guard dogs in addition to being a great pet. They are very loyal and protective of their owners, as well as being obedient and intelligent.

The German Shepherd breed needs a lot of exercise and activity. They are very active and strive to make their owners happy, however, they may not be very friendly to someone they do not know and might appear aloof at first. They may become overly protective of their family if they are not properly trained.

ARE GERMAN SHEPHERDS HEALTHY DOGS?

They can live to be about 10 years old, which is just about right for their size. One issue they may experience is they tend to have elbow and hip issues later during their life. In addition, their ears tend to get infected easily.

The next time you see a police officer with a K9 officer, think about how much training this dog has experienced and what his job duties include. Do not approach the K9 officer, but feel free to talk to the human officer about his amazing partner.

For additional information about police dogs, you can visit your local library, research the internet, and ask questions of your teachers, family, and friends.

Visit
petsunchained
(PETS & ANIMALS)
www.PetsUnchained.com
to download Free Pets Unchained eBooks
and view our catalog of new and exciting
Children's Books

Made in the USA
Monee, IL
05 February 2020

21356073R00040